I0622826

# The Savior
# and the
# Shadow Queen:
# A Fantastical Tale
# Told Through
# Sequential Poems

QUILLKEEPERS PRESS

Copyright © Kimberly McAfee, 2023
Book Cover Design by Quillkeepers Press
Edit by Dylan Webster and Stephanie Lamb
Format by Quillkeepers Press, LLC

*All rights reserved. No part of this book may be reproduced in any form or by any electronic or mechanical means, including information storage and retrieval systems, without the permission in writing from the publisher, except by a reviewer who may quote brief passages in a review.*

*This compilation contains some works of fiction. Locales and public names are sometimes used for atmospheric purposes. Any resemblance to actual people, living or dead, or to businesses, companies, events, institutions, or locales are completely coincidental. Any references to pop culture are owned by their specific companies and are not the property of the author.*

*There are some poems here within that represent thoughts of the author. Any resemblance to actual events, locals, or persons, living or dead, is entirely coincidental.*

*ISBN: 979-8-9868389-8-4*

Published by Quillkeepers Press, LLC
PO Box 10236
Casa Grande, AZ 85130

This book is dedicated to my mom

사랑해요, 어머니 ♥

If you or your loved ones are having suicidal thoughts, please contact the National Suicide Prevention Lifeline at 1-800-273-8255 (https://suicidepreventionlifeline.org/). If you are outside of the U.S., please visit https://www.befrienders.org for information.

# The Beginning

# The Players and Places

# The Current Time

# The Players Revisited

## The Real World

## A Year Later

## A Parting Message Just for You

# The Beginning

# Hands of Crimson

Her hands
Awash in warm
Deep red crimson
Pain pulsated throughout her body
A croak escaped her lips
A sound more akin
To an injured toad
Not the beautiful young woman
From whence it came
Everything blurred
She could see nothing but her red, red hands
Figures surrounded her
Their voices reduced to mumbling
Her breathing more labored
Horrible pain
Radiating from her arms
Unbearable
The end
Quickly approaching
All the while
Her hands still warm
From waves
Of deep red crimson

## Safe

Wrapped in freshly washed quilts
A room perfumed
By lovingly picked wildflowers
Alas, the injured maiden
Is now safe amongst loved ones
She hears a friendly voice
*Eselli? Can you hear me?*
Her childhood friend
Nabseatsi
A young man
Her eyes, now wide open
The pain in her arms
Now dull
Her wounds wrapped in
Fresh white bandages
The companions meet eyes
She hears the muffled voices
Of her parents
And the other Elders of the village
Eselli now knows
She is safe

## Council of Elders

There they sat
The leaders of the villages
Grave expressions
Washed over their faces

There sat
Eselli's father
The leader of the Warriors
Nabseatsi's father also
The leader of the Makers

The other leaders also there
All consumed
In their seriousness
They came from the other villages
The other villages
In the Great Valley

Leaders from
The Village of the Brewers
Who made drink
For merrier times
The Village of the Horsemen
Who breed and train horses
For all the villages

The Village of the Recordkeepers
Who record the laws
And correspond with other villages
Far away

These are all the leaders
All the villages
In the Great Valley

## An Imminent Threat

It was the Recordkeepers
Who told the others
Receiving correspondence
From the other villages

A war was upon us
Far away villages
Were being destroyed
Demolished
Into black smoke

The Shadow Queen
A terrible character
An enemy of old
Said to have deserted this land
Long ago
Driven away
By the Ancients of this land

She had returned with her Wraiths
Creatures who feast upon flesh
Devouring all in their wake
Whose form is akin
To fiery black smoke

Far away villages
Had been demolished
Eaten
The Queen and her Wraiths
With great speed
All had been turned to dust

She and her minions
Were moving
Faster and faster
Coming towards the other villages
Coming towards these villages
The villages in
The Great Valley

# The Players
# and
# Places

## Eselli

A sweet young maiden
Strong as she is beautiful
With skin milky white
Eyes of finely faceted onyx stone
Shining hair as dark as ebony wood

The daughter of the strongest warrior
A warrior herself
Brave and true
Kind-hearted and caring
Though
Headstrong and rebellious

But at her core
She was good
She loved her family
She loved her friends
She loved her tiny village
A life
Sweet and satisfying

# Nabseatsi

A fine young man
A heart of the finest gold
Kind and loyal
Swift and skillful

An ironmaker's son is he
With hair as brown
As freshly baked bread
His friendly eyes
The shade of firewood
Ready for kindle

A fine young man
A maker of the finest swords
He is as strong
As any of the brave warriors
Any village has to offer

An ironmaker's son is he
A lad of great character
Genuine
The greatest of friends
The hope of his village

## A Warriors Village:
## The Home of Eselli

The home of the Warriors
The bravest
The strongest
The most courageous
Of the Great Valley
And in all the land

They are known far and wide
For their victories
For their prowess
For their determination
They are the best of allies
And the most feared of foes

Skilled with axe
Hammers and hooks
Battering rams as well
This is home of the Warriors
The home of Eselli

## A Humble Little Village: The Home of Nabseatsi

The home of the Makers
All manner of crafts
Are perfected
In this tiny village

In this humble little village
You shall find
The finest swords
The most beautiful carvings
From freshly harvested wood

Bakers, weavers, dressmakers
All manner of crafts
Are offered here
The home of the Makers
The home of Nabseatsi

## The Shadow Queen

She wears armor
Of shining deep midnight
With silver nicks and dents
From many a brave warrior
Bested by
The Maiden of the Dark

No one has seen her face
How wretched it must be
Covered in scars and boils and blood
Blood of those she's slain
Ugliness unrivaled
How wretched it must be

She is evil
She is cruelty
She is hate
All gathered and personified in her

## The Wraiths

Beware the Wraiths, My Child
The servants of the Shadow Queen
They appear as fast-moving black smoke
Racing throughout the land
Leaving destruction in their wake
You see, no one knows what they are
Or from whence they came
Some say they are damned souls
Demons from the Underworld

They feast upon villages, My Child
Ravaging all in their path
Eating
Tearing
Screaming
Our terror is their delight
Claws and teeth are disguised
In that inky black smoke

All that is left behind, My Child
Is the dust
Dust of homes once filled
With laughter and love
Dust of villagers living their lives
Just like us

Dust of bright wildflowers
Picked for a first love
Dust of meals
Cooked with a mother's care

Beware the Wraiths, My Child
The servants of the Shadow Queen
They appear as fast-moving black smoke
Racing throughout the land
Leaving destruction in their wake
You see, no one knows what they are
Or from whence they came
Whether or not they are damned souls
They are the demons of this world

## Dark Destruction

Nothing but dust
Nothing but remnants
Of a life once lived

Overtaken
By the Shadow Queen
And her hungry Wraiths

Nothing remains
Nothing
Whole villages demolished

No bones to bury
No buildings to repair
Nothing but dust

## The Legend of The Weapon

It is something we all know
From birth it is told
A story
To help children off to slumber

It was left by the Ancients
Long, long ago
A strange riddle or even a *prophecy*
Weaved into many a creative
Bedtime story

No one knows what it means
For many, it is nothing more
Than a passing fantasy
Fit only
As imaginative fodder
For children's stories

## The Prophecy

Darkness and Chaos shall fall
Only one can end it
Many villages shall fall
Yet only one can end it

A Weapon in a sunless place
Deep within Mystic Mountain
Shall show the Truth
Only one can conquer the Darkness
Only one can be the Savior of this land
The Light shall come from the Truth

# The Current Time

## A Threat Grows Near

No more planning
No more strategizing
No more wondering
The war is upon us

Black smoke
Creeping upon the horizon
Darker
And darker still

If you are quiet
You can hear the Wraiths
Do they scream in pain
Or pleasure?

## The Warriors' Send-Off

They gathered round
The strongest of all the villages
In the Great Valley

The bravest and strongest
All had to offer
As well as the Great Warriors
Of Eselli's village

They were sent off with
Cheer and merriment
They were sure to win
These bravest and strongest
In the Great Valley

They would avenge
The villages destroyed
They would win this war
The Shadow Queen, no match
For warriors so brave and strong

## Uncertainty

Eselli and Nabseatsi
Noticed it straight away
The feeling

There had been Warriors' send-offs
Many before
But this was different
Strange

Times when they felt confident
Knew their loved ones would return
This war
An unparalleled war
Felt different
Strange

Eselli and Nabseatsi
Noticed it straight away
The feeling
Uncertainty

## The Warriors' March

On to battle!
We are the brave
We are the victorious
We will save this world

One foot in front of the other!
We march to glory
We march to defeat evil
We will restore good to the land

Onward we go!
We will extinguish the Dark
We will save the Light from this terror
We must win

*We must*

## Darkness on the Horizon

The villagers try to ignore it
No one dares to speak of it
The black smoke in the distance
The Darkness on the horizon

It's coming
It grows closer
The midnight that moves
So fast
Closer
Nearer than the day before

Everyone knows
Everyone sees
The sweat on their brows
Betrays their stoic faces

They all feel the terror
They all fear the worst
All the while
It comes closer
Closer
Nearer than the day before
The Darkness on the horizon

# The Hymn of the Wraiths

Praise be to the Shadow Queen
Who leads us to victory!
We shall feed
Upon flesh and fear
Running, running, running
We're coming
We're coming

We are as black smoke
To cover all the land
With Darkness pure
We move with stealth
We move with speed
Running, running, running
We're coming
We're coming

We shriek with delight
To gnaw on bones
To bathe in blood
Praise be to the Shadow Queen
Who leads us to victory!
Running, running, running
We're coming
We're coming

## Screams

Were those screams we heard
Were those the pitiful cries
From the bellies of
The bravest of our warriors?

No, that cannot be
Our bravest cannot be
Bested by mere black smoke

These are the finest
The Council of Elders
The strongest of our village
The most skilled of tacticians
All our finest warriors

No, those cannot be screams we heard
Our warriors are strong
The Greatest
Amongst all villages

No, that cannot be
Our bravest could never be
Bested by mere black smoke

## Waiting

Where are you,
    All our bravest warriors?
        Impatiently, we wait
            The black smoke couldn't best you,
                It never could!
                    Now return to us
                        and tell us of your triumph,
                            Greatest of all Warriors!

## A Warrior's Return

A figure
Comes upon the horizon
The villagers wait
Along with Eselli and Nabseatsi
With bated breath
The first of our warriors returns!
But the air felt different
Not cheerful
As other welcoming celebrations

They waited
Expecting to see the others
The others who have returned
Victorious
Gleeful
Strong and mighty
So many times before

There was only one
They waited
There must be more!
He must have
Led the way
For the flocks
Of our bravest warriors!

They waited
But no one joined
This solemn figure
They waited
But there was only one

## Terror

No one
Absolutely no one
Could have imagined
This terrible fate

There were doubts
There was
Fearful grumbling
But no one
Absolutely no one
Thought this could be
The outcome of it all

Hope extinguished
No one
Absolutely no one
Avoided
The overwhelming shock
Filled
With absolute terror
From the reality of it all

## A Light in the Darkness

Eselli and Nabseatsi
Filled with grief
Consoled each other

Their fathers now, like the other warriors
Gone
Killed by black smoke
Turned to dust
Like the many villagers before them

How could they fight
Murderous black smoke?

## Decisions

Could we be the heroes?
Could we help our people?
If no one else will stand,
Shall we?

Can a warrior's daughter,
Be as strong as the warrior himself?
Can a maker's son,
Make peace in the world?

## New Heroes Emerge

We shall be
The New Heroes
We shall be
The ones foretold in stories

We are but human
Young and inexperienced
But if not us
Then who?

We will defend
Our villages
We shall find
The Weapon
From the Prophecy
Of Ancients
We shall be
The New Heroes

## The Fool's Journey?

Their families
Their friends
Tried to stop them

*How could you leave now?*
*How could you go after something,*
*We don't even know is real?*
They asked Eselli and Nabseatsi

*We have no other choice,*
*But to try.*
*Shall we stay and succumb*
*To the Shadow Queen?*
Eselli and Nabseatsi rebutted

Their families
Their friends
Tried to stop them

There are times
One must leave
Go out on their own
And become the Hero they're meant to be

It may seem a fool's journey

But they had no choice
They had to try
To find the Weapon
To save their villages
What else could they do?

## A Fruitful Beginning

Loyal friends
From birth to young adulthood
Filled with promise
Filled with hope

We shall be the victors!
Eselli and Nabseatsi
The best of friends
Make the strongest warriors

Our adventure will be fruitful
We shall vindicate our brave ones!
Our warriors, our loved ones
Did not die in vain!

The beginning
Of the greatest adventure
To save our world
From the enveloping Darkness

## Onward to Mystic Mountain

Mystic Mountain
The place of magic
Worshipped by the Ancients
Home of the Weapon

It is a three days' journey
From the Great Valley
Our New Heroes
With speed and bravery
Must travel there

It is far, and it is difficult
But to stay
And succumb
To black smoke
That grows close is easy

Our New Heroes
They will run
Run with speed
With bravery
Until their sandals
Are reduced to threads
They will run
To save their villages

They will run
To Mystic Mountain
The place of magic
Worshipped by the Ancients
Home of the Weapon

## Almost Like Home

When I close my eyes
I can almost remember
Every sight
Every smell
The warmth of mother-made blankets

When I close my eyes
The smell
Of cooking provisions
Almost smells
Like delicious mother-made meals

When I close my eyes
I can almost remember
The village
My parents
The smiles of those I love

When I close my eyes
I am transported
To the reasons
We've embarked on this journey
Away from the cold
The hunger and the fear

When I close my eyes
I can imagine
When I close my eyes
It's almost like home

## Eselli Forgets

They ran and ran
Our young heroes
Eselli and Nabseatsi
Through glade and glen
Racing to the Weapon
Racing to save us all

Then she heard it
A sound so strange
Yet so familiar
Was it a bird? No
Something else
She was frightened
The journey suddenly coming to a halt

*Nabseatsi, did you hear it?*
*Did you hear the sound?*
*Not a bird…*
*…not a horse…*
*Not the scream of a man…*

*Eselli, you need to forget*
*It is nothing…*
*…you need to forget*
A look of concern and terror

Washing over his face
A look Eselli had not seen before

She was frightened
The noise continued
She tried to rebut
But Nabseatsi intervened
*No! It is nothing!*
*You must forget, Eselli!*
*We have an important journey!*

They continued on
Their journey renewed
Nabseatsi told her to forget
… And she did

## A Stranger on the Road

He was so nice
In the beginning
Eselli took a liking to him
Nabseatsi was cautious
With piercing blue eyes
Who made her heart go a-flutter

His name was Cerulean
Or so he said
They met him on the road
They told him of their journey
He was most
Enthusiastic

*I can help*
He said
*My village is near,*
*I can help you with provisions*
Cerulean offered
As they were running low
*It will not affect your journey at all*
He assured them

Against Nabseatsi's advice
Eselli agreed

*We shall leave in the morning*
Cerulean assured them
They sat around a fire
Cerulean telling stories
Eselli infatuated
Nabseatsi cautious

It happened
After they fell asleep
Eselli and Nabseatsi
In the morning
Cerulean was gone
He had stolen
Their provisions
Their small and humble provisions
Gone
While they slept

Eselli and Nabseatsi
Learned that day
Be wary of
A stranger on the road

## A Heavy Journey

Oh, how our mistakes
Make for heavy loads
Oh, how it makes
Walking through this world
So difficult
These weights on our shoulders

## The Cave

Through dangers and Darkness
The destination is found
Its wide mouth open
Ready to swallow them whole

Who has been here
Before our heroes?
Anyone?
Has a human foot
Ever touched
These sacred grounds?

The scene surrounding
Is pleasant
even sweet
Mountain and moss
Stone and wildflower
But at its center
A cavernous hole
Felled branches
And a cornucopia of vines
Cover the awaiting
Inky black inside

Though fear surrounds our heroes

Engulfs them
They tread on
Into the shadowy unknown
For the love of their families
For the future of their villages
For the future of the world
They trudge onward
To complete
Their hero's journey

## The Descent

Dark and dank
Dank and dark
A dreary scene

Through cobwebs
And shadowy creatures
Spiders and insects a-plenty

Our heroes
Make their way through
Torches in hand

Slippery rocks
Wet and covered in algae
Don't fall!
The air is cold
The stench
Of decay abounds

A subtle glow is ahead
Growing more pronounced
As Eselli and Nabseatsi approach

From the Home of the Warriors
From the Home of the Makers
Have we found
The Home of the Weapon?

## The Last Few Steps

It was there
In the middle of an open expanse
Deep in the ground

The cave sparkled
Dotted with quartz
Shimmering
Like bright night stars

Covered by old burlap
It was as tall as Eselli
Nabseatsi, too
What could this be?
It didn't move
Perfectly still

Anticipation swelled in Eselli
Her heart beating
Like ten thousand drums
She looked at her companion
He was calm
Deadly calm
She was frightened

Shining sand surrounded it

The Weapon
Soft and tan
Like an ocean's shore

They pressed their feet
Into the shining grains
Leaving mementos
Of their courage behind

*Remove the cloth, Eselli* whispered Nabseatsi
His voice
Odd, almost stern
His face
More serious
Than she had ever seen

Be brave
Eselli told herself
For our families
For our villages
For our future
She grabbed the burlap
…and ripped it away

## The Weapon(?)

There it stood
On a wooden stand
Long with sharp edges
Encased in wood

Eselli saw herself in it
She gasped at the sight
*I know this...* she whispered
Its name
On the tip of her tongue

She hadn't seen it in her village
Or in Nabseatsi's
She couldn't remember
Where she'd seen it
But it was familiar
All the same

As she took in
Her reflection
Nabseatsi stood still
Calm and quiet
Stern and silent
As if he were made of stone

*What is this?* Eselli asked
Unable to find its name
Nabseatsi's eyes
Turned to her
Their usual warmth
Replaced by
Weighty grayness

*You know what it is* he answered
*Something from another world,*
*A world you know all too well…*
Eselli was confused
She trembled with fear

*It is nothing to be afraid of* he continued
*Nothing of consequence…*
*A simple, everyday item…*
Nabseatsi then paused
*It is…*
*A mirror.*

## A Phantom Made Real

A wooden mask
Of pain and Dark sadness
Misery incarnate

Instead of Eselli
Looking back at herself
Suddenly there stood
The Shadow Queen
As she looked in the mirror

*What is this?* cried Eselli
Nabseatsi was calm
Expectant even
*Nothing to be afraid of…*
*Not anymore* said Nabseatsi

It was then the image
Began to move forward
Coming out of the mirror
Ripples like waves
Forming
Flowing
On the mirror's surface

*Run!* screamed Eselli

Certain doom approaching
Nabseatsi was still
Catching Eselli
Holding her in place
It was then
Eselli thought
She had been betrayed

Tears filled her eyes
All the while
The Shadow Queen made her way
Out of her glass prison

There she stood
Terrifying
Right before Eselli
And a seemingly treasonous Nabseatsi

The Shadow Queen
Began to move closer
It was then Eselli noticed
Blood dripping from the Queen's wrists
Onto the sparkling sand
Had she been wounded
From her escape?

Eselli was certain
Of imminent death
But instead of her sword
The Shadow Queen
The Dark One
The Destroyer
Reached for her mask
Pulling it off in one
Fell swoop

Eselli gasped
Not believing her eyes
The face
The face of the Shadow Queen
The face of terror and cruelty
Of misery incarnate
Was her own

## Written in the Sand

*It is time to remember*, said Nabseatsi
Stunned, confused
Eselli stood in silence
The shock
Too overwhelming

It is then
Nabseatsi
Her dear friend Nabseatsi
At least at one time
Began to write their names
His and hers
The greatest of friends
In the sand

She stared at them
What else was she to do?
What stranger situation
Could this be?
The Shadow Queen
A copy of herself
Standing by the wayside
This is a dream
A nightmare
Eselli thought to herself

Nabseatsi fixed his gaze
Upon his friend
Then, one by one
Crossed out a letter
Of his very name
And rewrote it in the sand

NABSEATSI

S – S
E – E
B – B
A – A
S – S
T – T
I – I
A – A
N – N

*Do you remember now?*
He asked Eselli
She could not understand
She could not fathom
This strange sight

He then proceeded
With her own name

ESELLI

L̶ – L
E̶ – E
S̶ – S
L̶ – L
I̶ – I
E̶ – E

When she saw it
Grief flooded her
Like roaring ocean waves
Sadness and shame
Guilt and remorse
So deep
Too much
Too painful to describe

Tears streamed down her cheeks
Like a heavy autumn rain
It was then she knew
It was then she remembered
Those names
Her friend's and her own
Written in the sand

## The Truth

This world
This fantastical world
Was not her own
None of it real

Her dear Nabseatsi
Her friend
Was gone
The image before her?
Simply a memory
Of a cherished companion

Her nemesis
The nemesis of all
The Shadow Queen
Was her
Her Darkness
Her self-hatred
Destroying her inner world
Like a militant tyrant

This world
Her village
Nabseatsi's village
All mere figments

Of her imagination
Composites
Of stories and movies
Fairytales and daydreams
Absorbed long ago

When she knew
When she remembered
Everything disappeared
Nabseatsi/Sebastian
The Shadow Queen/her Darkness
The cave
The Weapon
All gone
Nothing but stark white
Stark, shining white
Clean and sterile
Bright white

# The Players Revisited

## Leslie

A sweet girl
The best friend of Sebastian
Kind and adventurous
Brave and caring

She was the one
Who took the lead
She was the one
Always trying something new

Leslie, a young girl
A fireman's daughter
Her mother
A lawyer's paralegal

When college years came
She wanted to try
Many new things
Rebellious
Getting into trouble
Was just a new adventure

## Sebastian

A next-door neighbor
Kind and considerate
Warm and friendly

A best friend
Always there
Throughout the years

A responsible young man
Always there
To help a friend in need

A child of those who create
A baker and homemaker
An engineer

A ray of hope
An only child
The future of their lineage

## The Best of Friends

Hopscotch, giggle-filled afternoons, chalk drawings on the driveway, kindergarten, singing songs, cartoons, cereal prizes, chocolate chip cookies after school, first crushes, preteen awkwardness, sharing secrets, friendship bracelets, promising never to change, promising always to live next door to each other, high school, teenage angst, boyfriends, girlfriends, first loves, breakups, supporting each other through it all, homecoming, prom, graduation, ideas for the future, realizing the many changes and many more to come, colleges, partying, alcohol, responsibility, shirking responsibility, and all the complexities of being young.

BFFs

# Friendship Formed

A beautiful new house
A young family
A sweet little daughter
A time to build roots

A nice family next door
A young family
A kind little son
A time to build roots

A little boy
Yearning for friendship
A gift from the Universe
A little girl
A new friend

A game of hopscotch
A lonely little boy who played alone
A lonely little girl who wanted to play
A simple game
A friendship formed

## A Savior is Born

Sebastian was a sweet boy
Always kind
But other neighborhood kids
Bullies
They saw weakness instead
And tormented poor Sebastian

Leslie was protective of her friend
They played and visited each other
Every day
The others didn't pay her much attention
She was the "weird new girl"

She hated the taunts, the teasing
The rudeness to her new friend
Sebastian had sadly
Grown accustomed to
But not Leslie

She saw those taunts
The terrors that Sebastian endured
They pushed him to the ground
Calling him terrible names
With all her strength
She pushed them right back
She stood tall and defiant

These bullies had never
Been challenged
They were scared at the response
They didn't mess with Sebastian
After that
The "weird new girl" and her friend
Were left alone

                    And they did as they pleased

## Two

We, the best of friends
Two souls perfectly in sync
The Terrific Two

## Young Love

*I have a big crush on...*

*Oh really? I like...*

Boyfriends, girlfriends, best friends
Egging the other on
To make first love confessions
Double dates, happy moments,
Precious teenage memories

Heartbreak, flowing tears
The end of first love dreams
How fast beautiful moments
Can turn into heartache!
But best friends remain
A bond strong, of chosen family
A special kind of love

## Dreams of the Future

So many roads to take
So many ways to go
Maybe I'll go to college
What major shall I choose?
Will I meet my one true love
In Algebra I?
Maybe I could travel the world
By doing a study abroad?
So many ways to go
So many roads to take
Maybe I'll get a job
Work my way up the ranks
I don't think I want to go to college
I want to learn a craft
Maybe I'll meet my one true love at work
And we can have children right away
Who knows what the future will bring!
So many decisions
So many possibilities
But only one thing was certain:
Leslie and Sebastian
Would remain friends through it all

## An Unfortunate Event

She just needed a ride
Away
Away from the party
Away from
Her bad decision

Sebastian told her
Not to go
A wild party
Filled with strangers
Invited by an acquaintance
His name was Laurence
With piercing blue eyes
Who made her heart go a-flutter
It seemed awful sketchy

But Leslie
Headstrong and brave
A bit rebellious
Wanted to go
Wanted to try
Wanted to see

As she arrived
She knew it had been
A big mistake
There was alcohol
There were drugs
There were unfriendly faces
There were some
Too eager to be in her presence

She rode there
With her new "friend"
Who would not leave
Yelled at her for trying
To ruin a good time

It was then she left
Ran
Ran down the street
Aware of her
Bad decision

She tried to call a taxi
None were in the area
She couldn't call her parents

She'd be in so much trouble
She called Sebastian
Her best friend, BFF
He would help her, she knew
She called
He agreed
He would rescue her

But alas,
Some stories do not end well
On his way
Sebastian
Ready to save his friend
Had an accident
Someone ran a red light
A terrible crash
Leslie wasn't saved
And neither was Sebastian

## Guilt

overwhelmin*G*
       *U*nbearable
   suffer*I*ng
    aff*L*iction
  devas*T*ating

## Shame

I wake up
And you are there
I go to sleep
And still, you are there

You follow me
Day in, day out
Everyday
Is the same

You
A constant companion
This shame I carry

## I, Leslie

Have you ever been
Overtaken by self-hatred?
So deep that it could fill
An ocean
10,000 times over?

Have you ever been
Crushed by your own mistakes?
The weight so heavy
A million steel chains
Would be lighter

Have you ever been
Filled with deep regret?
Wishing, hoping, praying
All the mistakes
Had been but a dream?

Maybe you never have been
Consumed by such feelings
But I, Leslie, have

# The Accident

The thing you are never supposed to do
An act of desperation
I, Leslie did

# The Real World

## Awake

Leslie awoke
Eselli no more
No need for dreams
The Truth now revealed

The hospital
The room in which she lay
Stark and sterile
The walls bright white
So bright
They almost shine

Covered in blankets
The bed soft
Just as comfy
As Eselli's room in the village

Her hospital bed
Surrounded
By vases of flowers
And the scent of wildflowers
Green and sweet

There were also
Beeping machines
No birds, horses,
Nary a scream
She no longer had to forget

Her wrists covered
In stark white bandages
Covering her "accident"
Tears filled her eyes
Glad for another chance

## Unconditional Love

The love of a parent
Is unlike any other
Strong and self-sacrificial
Nurturing and protective
Forgiving and all-encompassing

Leslie's parents
Were filled with love and relief
No judgment
No criticism
Only love was present

Leslie knew
She had so much
So very much
To live for
For the love of a parent
Unconditional love
Was more than enough
The brightest star
Shining in the inky black Darkness
To lead her back
Back to her home

## Forgiveness

Sebastian's parents
Came shortly thereafter
Leslie was filled with fear

They could hate her
They *should* hate her
He was responsible and good
She was anything but

And then she saw them
Their eyes locked
There was no anger
Anywhere on their faces

As they came in
Tears streamed down their faces
Coming close to Leslie's bed
His mother grabbed her hand

There was no hate
Leslie gripped her hand tighter
And they cried together
Sobbing mightily

No words were spoken
None needed to be said
As everything was felt
Deep within their hearts

## Getting Help

It was then
She realized
She needed help

The doctors came in
To talk with her
About her "accident"

Monitored care
Was suggested
She needed help

She was ready
She wanted to be better
She needed help

Ready to feel better
Ready to improve her life
She was getting help

# Bravery

It is brave
To acknowledge you need help
And seek out mental health professionals

It is brave
To speak of your problems
With mental health professionals

It is brave
To follow a treatment plan
Given by those mental health professionals

Life is difficult
We are not machines
We all need help sometimes

It is true bravery
To acknowledge problems
To receive help
To follow treatment plans
Under the care of mental health professionals

# A Year Later

## To Forgive Oneself

Love yourself
    Empathize with yourself
        Try to understand yourself
            and your actions without judgment

Get help if you need it
    Oh, the world needs your bright and shining soul

## The Weapon/The Mirror

She gazed upon herself
In the large mirror
Alone
In a public bathroom

She made sure
Every hair was in place
Makeup
Perfectly applied

She was to have
An interview
A job
It was time

She was going
Through counseling
Healing
Becoming whole

She was nervous
But she was also
Strong
She had worked so hard

As she looked herself over
In her business suit
She could almost see
Nabseatsi
On her right
The Shadow Queen
On her left
Their hands resting
Upon her shoulders

They were always with her
To help her
Not a friend
Not an enemy
But part of her
Parts of herself
Representations of
The Light and the Dark within

She understood herself
She was strong
She grew
And was growing still

She smiled in the mirror

Once a devastating Weapon

She made her way

Towards the exit

Renewed

She made changes

She worked hard


…And Leslie was ready

## In Honor of Sebastian

I, Leslie
Will live
I will live a life
Happy and true
Honoring my family
Of blood and through friendship

I, Leslie
Will live
I will live a life
Sebastian would be
Proud of
That he, my friend,
My very best friend
Would want me to live

I, Leslie
Will live
I will live a life
Responsibly
No longer reckless
I will be the true warrior
He knew me to be
In my very soul

I, Leslie
Will live
I will live a life
That honors my friend
That honors his kindness
That honors his love
That honors his selflessness

I, Leslie
Will live
I will live a life
That honors
The greatest of warriors
The greatest of makers
I will live a life
In honor of Sebastian

## A New Beginning

There is always hope
        There is always a chance
                There is always a possibility
                        Of a new beginning

# A Parting Message Just for You

## You

You are strong
Stronger than you know
You are brave
Braver than you think

In this life
All manner of trials
Of tribulations
Shall make their way to you

There will be times
Your heart will be broken
Unfair situations
An ocean of tears
Shall make their way to you

There will be times
Your own mistakes
Will burden you
Heavy weights on your shoulders
Shall make their way to you

But know
Deep in your soul
That you can rise victorious

You can wear the winner's crown
No matter life's difficulties
You can rise up
And make a life
Sweet and satisfying

For you are strong
Stronger than you know
For you are brave
Braver than you think

If you or your loved ones are having suicidal thoughts, please contact the National Suicide Prevention Lifeline at 1-800-273-8255 (https://suicidepreventionlifeline.org/). If you are outside of the U.S., please visit https://www.befrienders.org for information.

# Special Thanks

First and foremost, thank you to my family! I love you all and am blessed beyond measure to have each of you in my life. Thank you for giving me the strength, support, and love to pursue my dreams. You guys are awesome, and I am thankful you're all in my life!

Thank you to my friends Serena Morrigan (@serena.morrigan on Instagram) and Enoch Black (https://stormdragonbooks.com/) for reviewing this book and for your meaningful suggestions. Because of the both of you, this book is a more robust piece of art. Thank you so much! I appreciate you both!

Big thanks to Stephanie Lamb, Dylan Webster, and the Quillkeepers Press team (@quillkeeperspress on Instagram) for publishing this book! You all have made a huge dream of mine come true, and it means so much to me. I am truly grateful for this opportunity! Thank you all very much!

Last but certainly not least, thank you for reading this book…and for sticking around to the *very* end! I hope you enjoyed this fantastical tale and that it has a positive impact on you. You are special and needed. Whatever mistakes you have made, you can rise above them and lead a meaningful life; a life that brings happiness to yourself and those around you. You are a piece of the world's puzzle; the world needs you in it ♥

# About the Author

Kimberly McAfee is a writer and poet residing in the US. She has authored/co-authored works in a variety of formats, such as websites, e-magazines, anthologies, and even a peer-reviewed scholarly journal. Ms. McAfee has a previous publication with Quillkeepers Press: *AmerAsian: My Journey to Becoming Whole as a Mixed Korean-American*. She has also self-published three chapbooks, available on Amazon. You can find more of her poetry on her Instagram page @writerpoetkim.

# What Others are Saying About
# The Savior
# And
# the Shadow Queen

"*The Savior and Shadow Queen* is a beautifully woven story, revealed one poem at a time, about one girl's journey towards acceptance and forgiveness after a mysterious Shadow Queen threatens to take everything away from her and her village. Kimberly tells a gripping story about loss and mental health in a heartfelt and thought-provoking manner that will leave the reader in a state of awe long after the last page has been turned."

— Serena Morrigan
Author of *A Song for Every Scar*

"Take a mystic and magical adventure with *The Savior and Shadow Queen*. This story is captivating, you get pulled into a enthralling world as you're going forth on a journey towards self-care and gratitude. The Shadow

Queen comes as a dark cloud, that makes it hard to see through the mist, to get to the other side. This mesmerizing tale about getting through grief and detriment, will have you questioning your mentalities. Reading this warms your heart and leaves you feeling full of the realization of having self-love."

— Gina Carrillo
Author of *Kaleidoscope* & *Poets United*

"*The Savior and the Shadow Queen: A Fantastical Tale Told Through Sequential Poems* by Kimberly McAfee is a stunning tapestry of poetry that draws you in from the beginning.

The characters are rich and lovingly described. Kimberly has taken her time to illustrate them in just a few stanzas. Eselli and Nabseatsi are characters that I instantly identified with and rooted for throughout. The Shadow Queen provides the ultimate antagonist with her Wraiths to do her bidding. With the introduction of The Prophecy and The Legend of the Weapon, you quickly turn the pages to see who and what will happen next. "Only one can conquer the Darkness.

Only one can be the Savior of this land." Wow, what a beautifully crafted set of lines.

The story kept me engaged, and I related to the overall theme of grief and heartache, which are palpable throughout. The book's last section is achingly beautiful, with twists and turns that will undoubtedly shock the reader, much like I was shocked. With an ending that is both somber and elegant.

I very much liked this book. It was such an emotional read of loss and friendship and, ultimately, redemption that Kimberly executed in an inspired way."

— Kim V. Poetry
Author of *Remember Me*

"*The Savior and the Shadow Queen* begins with a threat of tragedy as the Shadow Queen and her wraiths have been attacking nearby villages, leaving nothing behind. A young warrior, Eselli loves her village and sets out with her best friend Nabseatsi to find a weapon told about in legends that could defeat the Shadow Queen and save everything Eselli loves.

As the quest for deliverance is unfolded through poetry, a revelation brings the story closer to home not just for Eselli, but for the reader as well. *The Savior and the Shadow Queen* has a powerful message about friendship, forgiveness, and courage to face the things in life that seem insurmountable. While devouring shadows do pass into our lives, this beautiful tale reminds us we each have the power within to survive even our darkest days. This story and its message will linger in the hearts of all who read it."

— Michelle Wicklow
Author of *Woodland Spirits*

www.ingramcontent.com/pod-product-compliance
Lightning Source LLC
Chambersburg PA
CBHW030315130626
46549CB00002B/860